What Do I Do Now?

What Do I Do Now?

Practical Ways to Develop Good Behavior in Your Child

Alan M. Hofmeister, Ph.D.

Director
Outreach and Development Division
Exceptional Child Center
Utah State University

Charles Atkinson, Ed.D.

Associate Professor
Western Washington State College

Hester Henderson, M.Ed.

Staff Associate
Outreach and Development Division
Exceptional Child Center
Utah State University

ARGUS COMMUNICATIONS
Niles, Illinois 60648

Revised Edition

Printed in the United States of America.

ARGUS COMMUNICATIONS
7440 Natchez Avenue
Niles, Illinois 60648

International Standard Book Number: 0-89505-016-1
Library of Congress Number: 78-56863

0 9 8 7 6 5 4 3 2

Acknowledgements

Some of the ideas contained in this publication were adapted from earlier field test editions. Timm Vogelsberg, M.S., and Ann Porcella, M.Ed., assisted in the development and evaluation of these earlier editions.

CONTENTS

TALLY SHEETS AND GRAPHS   97

INTRODUCTION

Adults using the suggestions presented in this book may have to make changes to fit a particular child's age and interests. However, the basic methods presented should work with all children. Some of the activities may seem awkward at first, but they are not new. All of them have been used successfully with children.

Most children have *learned* to misbehave. The following shows how a child may learn to misbehave:

Adult: **What do you say, Johnny? Do you want to go home now?**

Child: No.

Adult: **Well, it's time, so get your coat.**

Child: I don't want to.

Adult: **Come on now, get your coat.**

Child: No.

Adult: **Johnny, get your coat *right now.***

Child: No.

Adult: **If you don't get your coat, I'm going to spank you.**

Child: (Crying.) No! No! I don't want to go home.

Adult: All right. Just stop crying. We can stay for five more minutes, but you have to stop crying right now.

Here is what the child might have learned from this exchange:

1. When grown-ups ask a question, I don't know if they want an answer or not. Sometimes they ask questions but really don't want an answer. It's very confusing.
2. If I say "No" to grown-ups, I get a lot more attention than if I just do what they tell me to do.
3. If I cry, I get to stay for five more minutes.
4. If I cry real hard, I won't get spanked.
5. If I cry loud enough, grown-ups will care more about getting me to stop crying than about spanking me or taking me home.

There are generally two types of questions concerning behavior that parents, teachers, and others who work with children ask: • "How do I get a child to do something?" and • "How do I get a child to stop doing something?"

This book is divided into two sections. The first section gives examples of *how to teach a child to behave*. The second section gives examples of *how to teach a child to stop misbehaving*. But before those examples are given, let us find out how to praise a child for good behavior, examine some basic rules for child discipline, and look at ways to keep track of what you are doing.

BEFORE YOU BEGIN

A NOTE ABOUT
PREVENTING MISBEHAVIOR

This volume is designed for any adult who wants to learn how to discipline a child. It discusses ways to teach appropriate behavior and to deal with misbehavior when it occurs.

The key to disciplining children is teaching them appropriate behavior before inappropriate behavior has a chance to occur. Since this is not always possible, we need to know how to deal with misbehavior when it does occur.

The method used here is simple. Basically, it is an attempt to replace misbehavior with good behavior. Here are some general rules to follow to help you teach children good behavior:

1. Watch for good behavior, and tell children what they are doing that you like. Never take good behavior for granted. We adults have a tendency to ignore good behavior and focus on misbehavior. Make a conscious effort to reverse that tendency. Teach children that your attention comes as a result of good behavior, not as a result of misbehavior.

2. Provide children with good models. Although this is not always possible, it is important to provide them with as many good models as you can. Try to expose them to playmates who are good "players," "workers," "learners," "talkers"—in other words, good at whatever behavior you would like the child to imitate. Avoid exposing children to

inappropriate models (that is, playmates or adults who consistently demonstrate inappropriate behavior).

3. Teach children how to behave by keeping them actively involved in situations that promote appropriate behavior. Provide them with a variety of stimulating activities, and praise them for playing and doing things in an appropriate way.

4. Prevent misbehavior by taking time to teach children how to behave. Play with them. Engage them in productive, enjoyable activities in which you can take part as well.

REINFORCEMENT

The kind of reinforcement referred to in this book is *positive reinforcement*. This type of reinforcement consists of attention and reward paid to a child for behaving, rather than attention and punishment for misbehaving. Positive reinforcement will tend to increase the behavior that preceded it.

Positive reinforcement may be in the form of *tangible rewards* or *social rewards*. Tangible rewards are objects that you give a child for good behavior. For example, if a young boy cleans his room, you might give him a cookie. If he rakes the leaves, you might buy him a toy. If he helps his little sister build a dollhouse, you might give him some ice cream. It should be noted here that there are a number of foods that

may serve as reinforcers. Some suggested treats include: fruits (fresh or dried) like grapes, apples, apricots, raisins; vegetables such as carrots or celery; nuts, cookies, etc. (Try to use the most nutritious foods you can. Replace rewards of food with social rewards as soon and as often as possible.) It might be useful to determine in advance what things are reinforcing to a particular child. What is reinforcing for one child is not necessarily reinforcing for another.

While tangible rewards can be an effective way to modify behavior, they may not always be desirable or available. Another type of positive reinforcement which works well and is free and easy to give is social rewards. These include any

behavior a person exhibits in an attempt to reinforce the good behavior of another. Smiling, touching, hugging, kissing, and patting are all examples of social reinforcers. So also are certain words and phrases such as: "You certainly are doing a good job, Edward" or "I like the way you are sharing with your sister."

The reinforcer we are probably most familiar with is praise. This book emphasizes the use of praise as an effective way to increase good behavior and decrease misbehavior.

Another method of modifying behavior is the use of a "quiet area" to deprive a child of positive reinforcement. If a child is misbehaving, an adult can often decrease that misbehavior by placing the child apart from others for one to five minutes immediately following the misbehavior. The child should be told why he or she is being isolated. This is frequently referred to as "time out." The "quiet area" is discussed more fully on page 23.

In learning to use reinforcement to increase good behavior, the adult must keep in mind several points:

1. *Notice when children are behaving.*
   Pay attention to children when they behave, and always reinforce them for it. Don't take good behavior for granted.

2. *Be specific in your praise.*
   Let children know exactly what it is that they did correctly.
   For example, "Very good" does not tell children exactly what they did. "Thank you for helping me set the table" would be a better comment. Some examples of things you might say to praise a child include:
   Wow! That's a very good picture you drew!
   Boy, you really set the table well.
   When you play nicely with the baby, I'm really proud of you.
   I like playing this game with you.
   Thank you for picking up your toys.
   You're doing just what I told you to do. I like that.
   You listened carefully. You did everything I said to do.
   I'm very proud of the way you ate dinner tonight.
   I've noticed you sit quietly watching TV. I'm so pleased with you when you do that.

3. *Reinforce immediately.*
   Try to reinforce children's behavior right away. Don't wait until after dinner to tell them they did a good job raking the leaves that afternoon.

4. *Reinforce small steps.*
   Reinforce small steps toward the desired behavior. For example, if you want to teach a little girl to wash her hands, you could start by praising her for going to the sink. After she has learned to go to the sink, you should show her the next step (turning on the water), then wait until she walks to the sink and turns on the water before reinforcing her. As the child learns to do one step, you can teach her another. The steps for washing hands would look like this:

Go to the sink.
Turn on the water.
Pick up the soap.
Wash the hands.
Rinse off the soap.
Put the soap in the holder.
Rinse the hands.
Turn off the water.
Dry the hands.

Praise the child for each step. When she learns one step, reinforce her and show her the next step. Wait until she can do both steps before reinforcing her again. By reinforcing small steps, you can teach a child to do things and to behave the way you like.

5. *Follow the three steps for teaching.*
Keep these three steps in mind when teaching a child something new:

TELL: Tell your daughter, for instance, how to do something. Then give her a chance to try it alone. Example: "Jane, go turn on the water. Just turn the handle."

SHOW: Show the child how to do something if just telling her isn't enough. Then give her a chance to try. Example: "Jane, this is how to turn on the water. Now you try it."

HELP: Help the child do something if showing isn't enough. Example: (Take Jane's hand and put it on the faucet.) "This is how we turn on the water, Jane." (Turn Jane's hand and the faucet until the water runs. Turn it off and give her a chance to try.) "Now, you try it."

Always praise children when they do a task.
Even if you help them, praise them for trying.
The goal is for children to be able to do
something alone when you tell them to.
You should insist that children be able to do
more and more each time on their own before
you extend praise. Remember the small steps
for washing the hands in number 4.

6. *Be consistent.*

   Whatever behavior you expect of children,
   continue to demand it. This is very
   important. Your responsibility is to let
   children know what you expect of them, and
   that you expect it today the same way you
   did yesterday. Children's responsibility is to
   make sure they follow the rules. For
   example, if the rule is "You get dessert only if
   you eat all of your dinner," then that rule
   should be enforced every day. Once you let a
   child get away with breaking rules, he or she
   will no longer believe in them. You must be
   consistent. It is often a good idea to let
   children help decide what the rules should be
   and what will happen if they are broken.
   That way they are as sure of the rules as
   you are.

7. *Ignore misbehavior.*

   Pay no attention to children's misbehavior
   whenever possible. Any kind of attention,
   even scolding, can be rewarding. Provided
   that the misbehavior is not harmful, ignoring
   it will often cause it to stop. When children
   get no attention for doing things that you

don't like, and plenty of attention for things that you do like, they will begin to do the things you like more often.

8. *Create a "quiet area" and use it when necessary.*
Sometimes a misbehavior is harmful and you cannot allow it to occur again. You may have warned a child and tried various distraction tactics. In that case you may need to use punishment. The "quiet area" is one form of punishment. A "quiet area" is a place where a child must stay for a limited amount of time (one to five minutes) with nothing to do. Merely associating with other people and being involved in what's going on is rewarding for a child. Removing him or her from activity and attention because of misbehavior is an effective way to stop that behavior. An example of a "quiet area" is a chair facing a blank wall. If a little boy is teasing his sister, for instance, you might have him sit in the "quiet area" for five minutes, then allow him to return to play.
A WORD OF CAUTION: The "quiet area" should be used sparingly to maintain its effectiveness. Use it only when other attempts to teach the child how to behave have not worked.

9. *Set conditions.*
Tell children that they must do something before they can have (or do) something that they really want. You should use this method when what you want a child to do is not absolutely necessary, and when you can wait

for the child to do it. Examples: "If you take off your coat and hang it up, we can read a book together." "When you put your toys away, you may have some juice." Be sure to state exactly what you want the child to do. You may need to use other cues to make sure he or she understands. For example, point to the coat and hanger or demonstrate putting the toys in their proper place.

10. *Make effective demands.*
   Sometimes what you want a child to do is absolutely necessary and cannot wait. In that case, using a statement such as "When you put on your jacket, I will give you a cookie" is not appropriate. A better statement would be: "It is time to put on your jacket. Please do so right away." Say it firmly. Do not confuse the child by mentioning a reward before he or she has obeyed you. And do not ask a question unless you are willing to accept a "Yes" or "No" answer. Asking a question when you are really making a demand can be confusing to a child. Some other rules for making demands are:
   Make only those demands that you can follow through on.
   Be sure the child knows how to do what you are demanding.
   Make sure the child understands. Pointing or demonstrating may be necessary.
   As soon as the child starts the task, offer praise.
   Be patient, and allow the child time to complete the task. Then give more praise.

If children do not do what they were told, firmly repeat the demand once. If they still do not begin the task, then help them physically. In the above example, you should begin by getting the jacket and starting to put it on the child. While you are helping, if the child does part of the chore alone, praise him or her immediately. Teach children that they will have to do what they are told one way or another.

Say nothing else. Only the demand and praise are necessary. Do not scold. Do not reason.

11. *Reason with a child only when he or she is behaving.*

Trying to reason with a child after misbehavior occurs can lead to many problems. Here is an example:

> **Adult:** **If you throw that clay one more time, you will have to leave the table.**
>
> **Child:** (Throws a ball of clay on the floor a few seconds later.)
>
> **Adult:** **I don't want you to throw clay because I have no time to clean it up.**
>
> **Child:** I'm sorry. I won't do it again.
>
> **Adult:** **You know I'm busy and can't waste my time picking up clay.**
>
> **Child:** I won't do it again.
>
> **Adult:** **Okay. But one more time, and that's it!**

What did the child learn about misbehaving? He or she may have learned, among other things:

Mom doesn't really mean it when she says I will have to leave the table if I throw clay. Mom is busy, but I want her to play with me. I'll throw the clay to get her attention. When I misbehave, all I have to do is say I'm sorry, and Mom will forget about it.

You should not try to reason with a child at a time like this. Wait until the youngster is being good. In this example, a good time to explain why clay must not be thrown is when the child is playing quietly with it.

REMEMBER:

1. Notice when children are behaving.
2. Be specific in your praise.
3. Reinforce immediately.
4. Reinforce small steps.
5. Follow the three steps for teaching.
6. Be consistent.
7. Ignore misbehavior.
8. Create a "quiet area" and use it when necessary.
9. Set conditions.
10. Make effective demands.
11. Reason with a child only when he or she is behaving.

IMPORTANT:

BE CONSISTENT ABOUT ALL RULES.

REINFORCE GOOD BEHAVIOR.

IGNORE BAD BEHAVIOR.

USE THE QUIET AREA
ONLY WHEN NECESSARY.

When you make a new rule for a child, be certain that the child understands the rule.

Example: "This is a new rule. If you hit your brother, you will have to sit by yourself for three minutes."

CHARTING BEHAVIOR

Charting a child's behavior is an effective way to tell if you are modifying it. It is also a good way to see if your rewards are working.

You can either chart behavior that you like or misbehavior that you dislike. When you begin to change a child's behavior, it may take a long time before you start to notice a difference. For example, if Anita hangs up her coat once a day when she had not been hanging it up at all, you may not notice the improvement right away. But if you had a chart—a record of the times Anita hung up her coat—you would know that she was behaving acceptably more often. Sometimes this is the only way to see that what you are doing is working.

Observe and chart the child's behavior for one week without doing anything else about it. You can then compare the first week's chart with those of following weeks. If you are changing the child's behavior, it will show on the charts. Behavior that you are trying to promote should show an increase on the charts. Misbehavior that you are trying to discourage should show a decrease on the charts. It should be noted, however, that ignoring misbehavior will often cause it to increase at first, before it decreases.

You should keep a record of a child's behavior on a tally sheet, and then make a graph (by days or weeks). Some children like to see the graph and help draw the lines.

An example of a tally sheet appears below. You will need a tally sheet to make daily or weekly graphs. (See pages 97–104 for blank tally sheets and graphs.) An example of a graph-by-days appears on page 32. An example of a graph-by-weeks appears on page 33.

Tally Sheet

In using a tally sheet, you record the number of times a child exhibits a certain behavior. On the sheet below, you can see that during the week of February 3–9, the child behaved in a certain way four times on Monday, five times on Tuesday, six times on Wednesday, etc. The first week, the child behaved that way thirty-two times, the second week twenty-seven times, the third week twenty-four times. From a daily or weekly record, you can tell if a child is exhibiting a certain behavior more or less often.

TALLY SHEET

	DATES	MON	TUE	WED	THUR	FRI	SAT	SUN	TOTAL
	FEB 3–9	IIII	JHT	JHTI	IIII	JHT	IIII	IIII	32
	FEB 10–16	IIII	III	IIII	JHT	IIII	IIII	III	27
	FEB 17–23	III	IIII	III	IIII	III	III	IIII	24

Number Of Times The Behavior Occurs

Graph-by-Days

From a tally sheet, it is easy to make a graph. On Monday the behavior occurred four times, so put an "X" at the "4" above Monday. On Tuesday the behavior occurred five times, so put an "X" at the "5" above Tuesday. Continue graphing the number of times for each day. Draw a line to connect the "Xs" on the graph, so that you can see the general pattern of behavior.

In most cases, graphing behavior by days takes a good deal of time and paper. Graphing by the week is usually more efficient, and it gives a better picture of the patterns of behavior over a period of time. An example of a graph-by-weeks is shown on the next page.

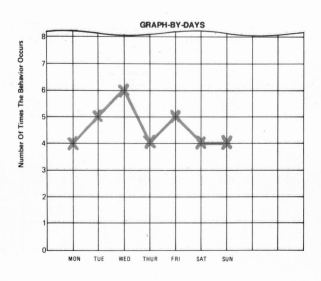

Graph-by-Weeks

A weekly graph is also made from a tally sheet. During the first week (February 3–9), the behavior occurred thirty-two times. Put an "X" at "32" above February 3–9. In the second week (February 10–16), the behavior occurred twenty-seven times. Put an "X" at the "27" above February 10–16. In the third week (February 17–23), the behavior occurred twenty-four times. Put an "X" at the "24" above February 17–23. Draw a line to connect the "Xs" on the graph, so that you can see the general pattern of the behavior. This graph shows us that the behavior has decreased from thirty-two times a week to twenty-seven times a week to twenty-four times a week.

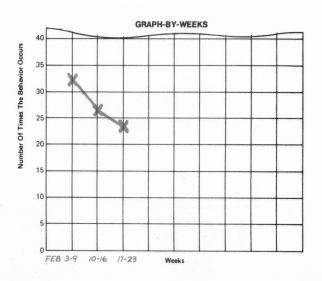

33

How to Use Examples:

The two sections that follow give specific examples of how to modify a child's behavior. The first section (pages 35–62) shows ways of teaching a child to behave. The second section (pages 63–95) shows how you can teach a child to stop misbehaving. The examples are written in this form:

A: This is what the adult says.

A: (This is what the adult does.)

C: This is what the child says.

C: (This is what the child does.)

TEACHING A CHILD
TO BEHAVE

FOLLOWING DIRECTIONS

It is important for children to learn to follow directions. To do this, they may often need to improve their listening skills. These are suggestions for teaching a child to listen and to follow directions:

1. Say the child's name. Wait for eye contact, then praise the child for paying attention. When he or she looks up at you, give the directions and ask that they be repeated.

2. Whenever the child follows a direction correctly, give praise immediately. For example: "Thank you for rinsing off your dish and putting it in the sink. You did that just the way I asked."

3. Avoid saying "You don't listen" or "That's not what I told you to do!" Ignore mistakes whenever possible, and praise the child when directions are followed.

4. You can also make a game of learning to follow directions. Hide a nickel (or something the child likes) somewhere in a room. Tell the child to listen to your directions and follow them *exactly* in order to find the nickel. Give directions *only once.* For example:

   A: (Hides a nickel.) **Freddie, you may have a nickel if you listen to my directions and follow them exactly. Go to the**

**kitchen. Open the top drawer next to
the sink.**

NOTE: Do not repeat directions.

C: (Follows directions exactly.)

**A: Take the nickel from the back of the
drawer.**
(Notice that in order to keep the nickel,
the child must go straight to the kitchen,
pull open the top drawer next to the sink,
and look in the back of the drawer. If he or
she goes to another drawer or makes any
other mistake, the child may not have the
nickel. You may want to hide the object in
a new place and give new directions.
If the child follows the directions exactly,
be sure to give praise. You might make an
additional reward by hiding another nickel
or other object.)

REMEMBER: Give the directions only
once! Start with very simple directions.
Then, as the child gets better at following
them, make them longer and more
complicated. Be sure that the directions
are clear and easy to understand.

It is a serious error to punish so-called
misbehavior that results from misunderstanding.
For example, if a parent says to a small son,
"Play with your toys after you put on your

slippers," the child might immediately start playing with his toys because he did not understand the meaning of "after" or because he only heard the first part of the instruction. The meaning might have been clarified by giving two separate instructions: "Put on your slippers." (Child obeys and receives praise.) Then, "Now you may play with your toys." Another way to simplify the instruction is to put the two activities in their proper order: "Put on your slippers, then play with your toys."

Adult Dialog

EXAMPLE 1   Praising and rewarding for following directions.

A: **Billy!**
(Waits until Billy makes eye contact.)
Thank you for paying attention. Please put on your boots and mittens and come outside with me.

C: (Puts on his boots and mittens and goes outside with the adult.)

A: **You really listened well, Billy. You quickly put on your boots and mittens and came outside. Let's take the dog for a walk. Then we can make hot chocolate when we come home.**

EXAMPLE 2   Praising for following one direction; ignoring mistakes.

A: **Suzy!**
(Waits until Suzy looks up.)
**Listen carefully. Please take off your
boots and put them on the back porch.**

C: (Takes off her boots and leaves them on the floor.)

A: **Suzy, thank you for taking off your boots
so quickly. Now please put them on the
back porch.**

C: (Puts her boots on the back porch.)

A: **Thank you for putting your boots on the
back porch.**

EXAMPLE 3   Praising and rewarding
for following directions.

A: **Jim!**
(Waits until Jim looks up.)
**If you will do exactly as I tell you, we will
go to the store when you're finished.**

C: Good! What do you want me to do?

A: **Please take all the newspapers and put
them on the garage shelf. Then sweep
the garage floor.**

C: Sure, Dad.
(Takes out all the newspapers and puts them
on the garage shelf. Sweeps the garage floor.)

A: **Good job, Jim. Thanks for following my
directions. Let's go to the store now.**

PAYING ATTENTION

If a child has trouble paying attention to what you say or to what he or she should be doing, follow these basic rules:

1. Notice when the child *is* paying attention to what he or she is doing. Offer praise immediately: "I like the way you are working hard" or "You are really paying attention. That's great!" You might even reward the child with a special treat.

2. Whenever the child *is not* paying attention, ignore him or her. Do not say "You aren't listening" or "You aren't doing your work" or "Sit down here and get to work!" Give attention only when the child *is* paying attention.

3. For children who *always* have trouble paying attention, it may be helpful to use a kitchen timer or a small egg timer. When you want children to work, set the timer for three minutes. If using an egg timer, turn it over so the sand can run through. Tell children that if they pay attention to their work for three minutes, they may then do something they like for three minutes. Be sure to praise children for paying attention. You should gradually increase the time children must pay attention.

Adult Dialog

EXAMPLE 1 Praising for paying attention.

A&C: (Sit down to work on a puzzle.)

C: (Starts finding pieces.)

A: It looks as though you are eager to put this puzzle together. I like the way you are working on it.

A&C: (Work together for five minutes.)

A: You are working so hard today. We are almost finished!

EXAMPLE 2 Ignoring; praising; setting conditions.

A: (Starts to help child with homework.)

C: (Stops and stares out the window.)

A: (Ignores child.)

C: (Gets back to work.)

A: It looks as if you're ready to work hard now. As soon as we're finished, you may turn on the television.

C: Hurrah!

EXAMPLE 3 Setting conditions; praising.

C: (Sits down to write out spelling words.)

A: Today we'll use an egg timer while you work. If you work on your spelling until the sand runs through, we'll turn over the egg timer and you may look at your comic book until the sand runs through again. Then you will go back to work on your spelling.

C: (Turns over the egg timer and works on spelling until the sand runs through. Then turns timer over again and looks at comic book. When the sand runs through once more, child goes back to working on spelling.)

A: Very good! You are paying attention to your work.

PICKING UP TOYS

Children often fail to pick up their toys, making extra work for adults. One way to handle this problem is to deny the child the use of those toys for a period of time.

1. Get a large box, such as a grocer's cardboard box. Tell the child that toys left lying around will be put in that box.

2. Anything put in the box may not be removed until the following day or until a particular day like Saturday or Sunday.

3. You may help motivate the child by counting the number of toys that are put in the box during the first week. Offer him or her a special treat or privilege at the end of the

second week if there are fewer toys in the box. At the end of each week there should be fewer and fewer toys in the box.

4. Since the purpose is to teach the child to be tidy, it is important to offer praise when he or she does pick up the toys.

5. The advantage of this system is that it eliminates the need for nagging: "Howard, pick up your toys!" Once the box idea is established, you can stop reminding the child about picking up. The responsibility has now become the child's.

Adult Dialog

EXAMPLE 1   Using box; ignoring arguments.

C: (Finishes playing with blocks and goes off to watch television, leaving blocks scattered on floor.)

A: (Notices blocks after child has gone to bed. Picks them up and puts them in the box.)

C: (Next day.) Where are my blocks?

A: You left them lying on the floor, so I put them in the box.

C: That isn't fair!

A: You may have them back tomorrow morning.
(Ignore all argument. See the "Arguing" section on page 64.)

EXAMPLE 2   Praising for picking up toys.

C: (Finishes playing with blocks and puts them into proper container. Puts container away on shelf.)

A: **I'm pleased that you are remembering to put away your toys.**
(Hugs the child.)

C: Yeah! I don't want them in that box again. I like those blocks. I'm going outside to play now.

A: **Have a good time!**

EXAMPLE 3   Using special privileges as reward.

A: **It's Saturday, so you may take your toys out of the box and put them away.**

C: Oh, boy! You said I could go swimming today if I have less than six toys in the box.
(Goes to box, takes out toys, and counts them.)
I only have *four* toys in the box!

A: **That's great! That shows you are really learning to pick up your things. Let's go swimming now!**

PLAYING WITH OTHER CHILDREN

Some children are happy playing by themselves or with others. They are both self-sufficient and social.

Other children keep playmates away by misbehaving—hitting, arguing, interrupting, teasing, or not sharing. You can teach such a child acceptable behavior by reading the sections in this book that deal with those problems.

Many children, however, would like to play with others but are afraid, shy, or unsure of themselves. They may not know how to play with other children. If a child is too shy or doesn't know how to play with others, follow these rules:

1. Be conscious of the child's feelings. For instance, if you take a child someplace where he or she has the opportunity to play with another child, watch them. If your child is

hesitant and afraid to play, gradually build his or her confidence so that he or she can interact with others.

2. When you are with the child and he or she smiles at or talks with another child, offer praise for being friendly. You might even try playing with both children for a while.

3. Be careful not to push the child into uncomfortable situations. If the child is shy, large groups of children may be threatening at first. Try to find one child to play with him or her. If that goes well, the child may soon be ready to play with several children.

4. Let the child know that you care. Comfort the child if his or her feelings get hurt while playing, but don't be overprotective. Children can be cruel to one another. So every child has to learn that some playmates are fun, and some may have to be avoided or ignored. Help the child learn to distinguish.

Adult Dialog

EXAMPLE 1   Teaching child how to play with others.

C: (Is playing alone in backyard. New next-door neighbors' son is also playing alone in his backyard. Looks at neighbor with interest.)

A: (Calls over to neighbors' child.)
Tommy, ask your mother if you may

**come over to our backyard. Let's all
three play a game together.**
(Plays with both children for a short time.
Then finds a reason to leave.)
**I have to check the laundry now. You
play without me for a while.**
(Starts out with very short periods, then
makes them longer and longer.)
You are playing well together. I like that.

EXAMPLE 2   Not pushing child into
uncomfortable situations.

(You and your little girl are at a social
gathering. A number of parents and children
are present, and your child is nervous.
Someone suggests you let her go outside and
play with the other children.)

A: **Ann, you may go out and play with the
other children, or you may sit quietly
with me.**

C: I don't want to go outside.

A: **Very well. You may stay here.**

EXAMPLE 3   Noticing child helping others;
praising.

C: (Helps little brother pick up toys and put
them away.)

A: **That is really nice. I like to see you
working together.**

SHARING

Children are often afraid to share, either because others have not shared with them or they fear they may lose their belongings.

1. Whenever you have a chance, share something of yours with children. This includes allowing them to use something of yours. It also includes encouraging them to help you do something they enjoy (cooking, planting a garden, making repairs). Children will learn from these experiences that you trust them with your things and that you also trust them to do a good job.

2. When children use something of yours, praise them for holding or using it correctly.

3. Whenever children share their possessions with anyone, thank or praise them. "Thank

you for letting me read your book. I will take good care of it. It is very nice of you to share it with me."

4. When children start sharing with you, do not keep their belongings very long. Give them back quickly, and say, "Thank you." As children become more relaxed and willing to share, they won't mind if you keep their things for longer periods of time.

5. Never scold or force children to share. They will only feel resentful, and will be even less willing to share. Instead, always praise them for sharing. Help them feel generous by sharing your praise with them.

Adult Dialog

EXAMPLE 1   Sharing with child.

A: I'm going to make some cookies now, Jimmy. Would you like to help me?

C: Yes! Can I lick the spoon?

A: Certainly.

A&C: (Measure ingredients together.)

A: You're really measuring carefully. I'm glad you're helping me today.

EXAMPLE 2   Sharing for a short time.

C: (Is playing with new truck.)

A: That's a nice truck. May I look at it?

C: (Reluctantly.) Well . . . okay.

A: (Takes truck and admires it. Gives it back after a few seconds.)
Thank you for sharing with me. I liked looking at your truck.

EXAMPLE 3   Not forcing child to share.

C: (Is playing with new doll.)

A: **You really like your new doll, don't you?**

C: Uh huh.

A: **I can tell you like it because you take such good care of it. May I hold it for a minute?**

C: No! (Hugs doll closely.)

A: (Casually.) **All right. Maybe you'll want to show it to me later.**

SITTING STILL

Children who are always moving about and acting restless can present a problem. Such behavior might occur because those children want attention or because you fail to notice and comment on the times when they *are* quiet. To lengthen the time children can sit still, you must become conscious of their behavior. You must help them create times of peace and quiet, which all children need.

1. When children are being overly active, try to ignore them. This is difficult, but it is important not to give undue attention to such behavior.

2. When children *are* paying attention and sitting still (or at least not jumping about), be sure you praise them. It is important to notice when a child is quiet. His or her overactive behavior may be a bid for your attention.

3. An egg timer or other type of timer may be used to help children sit still for longer periods of time. Set the timer near children (but out of reach), and tell them that they are to sit still for a short period of time (one to three minutes at first). Be sure they have things to keep them busy. You can make this into a kind of game. Begin to chart how long children sit still, and show them how they are doing. When they manage to sit still for the desired length of time, reward them. Have

children set their own limits of how long they will sit still. They will try harder to meet self-imposed limits.

4. You can make contracts with children. For example, say: "If you can sit still for one minute and work with your picture cards, I'll give you some milk and cookies." If children fail to keep their contracts, they forgo the treat. If they succeed, they receive a reward.

Adult Dialog

EXAMPLE 1   Praising for sitting still.

C: (Is sitting quietly and working on a puzzle.)

A: Thank you for working on your puzzle so quietly. I really like to see you working hard on something. Would you like me to help you?

C: Yes. I'm having trouble with this piece.

EXAMPLE 2   Setting conditions; praising.

C: (Is trying to work in a coloring book, but is restless and cannot stay with it.)

A: If you work in your coloring book for one minute, I'll go for a walk with you.

C: (Colors a picture quietly for one minute.)

A: You are really trying. You worked hard on that picture. Let's take a nice walk together.

EXAMPLE 3   Using a timer.

A: (Shows timer to child.)
See this timer? I want to find out how long you can sit still and look at your storybook. How long do you think you can do that?

C: I don't know. Maybe a minute?

A: Okay. Let's set the timer for one minute. I'll put it where you can see it.
(Explains how to tell when time is up.)

C: (Looks at storybook for one minute.)

A: That's very good. You looked at your book quietly for a whole minute. Let's keep a record of how long you can sit and work quietly.
(Keeps track of how long the child can sit still. After the child has sat still for one minute three times in a row, increase the time.)

TAKING CARE OF THINGS

If children often break their own or other people's things, follow these rules:

1. Tell a child: "It is good to take care of your things. It is good to take care of other people's things, too."

   Pick up something that belongs to the child—something that he or she likes very much.

   "This is your record player. You like your record player very much. You want to take good care of it, so you will have it for a long time. I want to take good care of it, too, because it belongs to you."

   Pick up something that belongs to you and that you like very much.

   "This is my knitting bag. I like my knitting bag. I want to take good care of it. I want *you* to take good care of it *too*, for me."

   REMEMBER: Do not reason with a child right after misbehavior. It serves only to call attention to what he or she did. Reason with children when you find them taking care of things.

2. You must praise children every time you see them handling something carefully or taking care of their own or someone else's property. Be specific in your praise: "I can see that you are holding that glass very carefully" or "You

are showing me that you respect my toolbox because you used it carefully. Thank you." Follow your praise with a hug.

3. Once children start taking better care of their own and other people's things, reward them with something new.

4. If you find children breaking things, quietly remove the objects. Explain that when they break things, they must go to the "quiet area." (See page 23.) Leave them there for one to three minutes or until they have been quiet for one to three minutes. In some cases you might tell children that they will have to do jobs to earn the money to pay for what has been broken. See that these jobs are done on a regular basis and as soon as possible. It is important that children learn to be responsible for their actions.

Adult Dialog

EXAMPLE 1   Praising for taking care of things.

C: (Doing a jigsaw puzzle. Has difficulty making one piece fit.)

A: That looks like a hard piece.

C: It won't fit!

A: It's really giving you a lot of trouble, isn't it? Maybe we can do it together.

C: Okay. (Hands puzzle piece to adult.)

A: You're taking good care of this puzzle. Does the piece go this way?
(Turns piece in correct direction.)

C: I guess so. Thanks.
(Puts piece in place.)

A: Thank *you* for taking care of the puzzle.

EXAMPLE 2   Rewarding with something new.

(A week has passed, and the chart shows that Tommy hasn't broken anything deliberately.)

A: I've bought you something new because I've noticed that you've been taking good care of things.

C: Oh, boy!

EXAMPLE 3   Sending to "quiet area" for deliberately breaking things.

C: (Is drawing a picture with pencil. Pencil lead breaks. Child breaks pencil and throws it across room.)

A: You may not break things. You must go to the "quiet area" for three minutes.
(Says nothing further. Sends or takes child to "quiet area.")

WORKING

Some children have to be told over and over again to work at something. When this happens, the child is controlling the adult. Some children will say "No" whenever you ask them to do a job.

1. When children are working on something (for you or for themselves), be sure to praise them. If you praise them for doing jobs, they should start enjoying the activities and look forward to getting praised.

2. When children refuse to work, it may be because they have not been noticed or praised for working. Ask children to work with you on something that they enjoy doing. When they do it, praise them.

3. Try to get children to work on things that they have refused to do before. Don't ask too much at first. You may have to praise them for small steps in the beginning. If children just look at what you want them to do, you might say: "Good. You are paying attention. Now pick up your clothes." Sometimes praising small steps will encourage a child to do the task.

4. Some children like to work toward a goal. Tell them that they may have a certain reward if they do something: "If you will help clear the table, you may invite Peggy over to play for a while."

5. If children refuse to do a job, explain that this is not allowed and they will have to go to the "quiet area." The "quiet area" should be used infrequently, and children should be immediately directed back to the work situation.

6. You may need to help a child for a week or more before you begin getting results. But if you are consistent, praise will teach the child how to work.

Adult Dialog

EXAMPLE 1   Praising small steps.

A: (Is sitting at the dinner table.)
**Mary, take your plate to the sink,
please.**

C: (Looks at her plate, but does not remove
it.)

**A: Thank you, Mary, for paying
attention. Now pick up your plate.**

C: (Picks up plate.)

**A: Good. You picked up your plate. Now
take your plate out to the sink and I
will take mine.**

A&C: (Take plates to the kitchen sink.)

A: I really like it when you work with me.

EXAMPLE 2   Setting conditions.

A: (Is sitting at the dinner table.)
**Hank, if you take your plate to the
sink, you may have dessert.**

C: (Looks at his plate, but does not remove
it.)

A: (Serves dessert to those who have
removed their plates.)
**When you take your plate to the sink,
Hank, you may have dessert, too.**
(Do not give the child any dessert until he
takes his plate to the sink. He may go

without dessert rather than obey you.
Or he may go without dessert for several
days until his favorite is served.
Eventually, he will take his plate to the
sink in order to get dessert. When he
does, praise him.)

EXAMPLE 3   Using "quiet area."

A: (Is teaching child to pick up clothing.)
Joan, please pick up your clothes.

C: No, I don't want to.

A: **If you won't do that job for me, you
will have to go to the "quiet area."**
(Takes child to "quiet area.")
You must sit quietly for one minute.
(After the child has remained quiet for
one minute, return her to the task of
picking up clothes. If she still refuses,
take her back to the "quiet area" or
follow the *Tell, Show, Help* procedures
on page 21.)

TEACHING A CHILD TO STOP MISBEHAVING

ARGUING

The child who continually argues is usually either trying to get attention or attempting to get out of doing something. Here are some rules to help you deal with an argumentative child:

1. Establish a rule about arguing: "We don't seem to get anywhere arguing. I'm not going to argue with you anymore."

2. If a child starts to argue after you have refused a request, say nothing further. Go on about your business, and do not look at the child or say a word. Do not encourage arguing by paying attention to it.

3. If the child starts to argue after being told to do something, repeat the demand firmly. If the child still argues, ignore what he or she is saying and physically help with the task.

4. When a child does *not* argue, give praise right away. Say: "Thank you for getting ready for bed" or "That's good. You did not beg for another cookie when I told you 'No.'" Follow immediately with a hug.

Adult Dialog

EXAMPLE 1   Being consistent; ignoring; helping; praising.

A: Okay, John. It is time to go to bed.

C: I don't want to go!

A: John, it is time to go to bed.

C: I'm watching TV.

A: (Firmly directs child toward bedroom, ignoring protests. Gets out pajamas.)
Put on your pajamas.

C: (Begins undressing.)

A: **I like the way you are obeying me. That is really good.**

C: (Puts on pajamas.)

A: **Good night, John. I am proud of the way you got ready for bed.**

EXAMPLE 2   Setting conditions; ignoring; praising.

A: **I'm setting the timer now. In five minutes you will have to go to bed.**

C: No! I don't want to go!

A: (Ignores child and continues setting timer. In five minutes, timer rings.)
There's the bell. Time for bed.

C: Aw, shoot! (Goes to bedroom, puts on pajamas, and gets into bed.)

A: **I like the way you went to bed when the bell rang. I'm proud of you.**

EXAMPLE 3   Setting conditions; praising.

A: **Sally, if you put your pajamas on and get into bed without complaining, I'll read you a story.**

C: Oh, goody! (Puts on pajamas, and goes to bed.)

A: **Sally, you are great at going to bed without complaining. I'll read your story now.**

EXAMPLE 4   Setting conditions; making demands; being consistent; ignoring.

A: **Roger, if you put your pajamas on and get into bed without complaining, I'll read a story from your new book.**

C: I don't want to go to bed. I don't care about a story.

A: (Ignores child for two or three minutes.) **Okay, Roger, go get into bed.**

C: No, no, no!

A: (Firmly.) **Roger! Listen! Go to bed right now.**
(Uses physical help if necessary.)

C: (Gets into bed.)

A: **Good night, Roger.**

C: What about my story?
(Cries.) I want a story!

A: (Ignores child and leaves the room.)

GETTING INTO EVERYTHING

Some children seem to be constantly getting into everything. They go from place to place, always leaving a mess behind. Such children may have short attention spans and may need to learn how to concentrate better. They may also need to be taught to put things away and keep their hands off things that do not belong to them. You can help children by following these suggestions:

1. Praise children every time they use something and put it away.

2. Do not give attention to children when they are getting into things. Avoid saying "Why can't you leave things alone?" or "You are always getting into everything."

3. Spend a few minutes every day with children exploring things that seem to interest them. For example, if a child likes to get into the button box, suggest getting it out. Dump all the buttons onto the floor, sit down with the child, and look at the buttons together. Talk about the buttons, handle them, and *enjoy* this activity with the child. Help him or her increase attention span by calling attention to shapes and colors. Show how buttons can be sorted by color or shape or size or other means.

4. When a child shows signs of tiring, say: "Well, I guess we are through looking at the buttons.

Let's see how fast we can put them back in the box. Then we'll eat lunch."

5. Be sure to praise the child: "I like the way you picked up those buttons."

Adult Dialog

EXAMPLE 1   Praising for putting things away.

C: (Walks past cupboard where brooms and other cleaning items are kept. Stops, opens cupboard, looks in, and takes out broom. Pushes it from side to side a few times, then puts it back in cupboard.)

A: **Thanks for putting away the broom, Billy. It's good to put things away when we're finished with them.**

EXAMPLE 2   Helping increase attention span.

C: (Is wandering around living room.)

A: **Let's take out some magazines and look at them.**
(Goes to bookshelf and takes out a few magazines.)
You take some, too, and we'll look at them together.

C: (Helps pull out magazines.)

A: **That's good. Now we can sit down and look at them, can't we?**

A&C: (Look at magazines together. Adult points to pictures of interest, asks child questions about them, and responds to child's comments and questions.)

C: (Starts getting bored.)

A: **You're tired of looking at the magazines, I guess. We can put them back now. Then we can play a game or work on something you like.**

A&C: (Pick up and put away all magazines.)

A: **Boy! You picked up all those magazines. You really did a good job!**

EXAMPLE 3 Ignoring and praising.

C: (Opens kitchen drawer and takes out measuring cups. Starts playing with them, then leaves them on counter.)

A: (Ignores child leaving cups on counter.)

C: (Picks up egg timer and turns it over to watch the sand run through. Puts timer back on shelf.)

A: Thanks for putting back the timer, Becky. I like that.

HITTING

Hitting is usually a way of attracting attention or getting one's own way.

1. Whenever children do *not* hit someone when angry, be sure to praise them. Say: "I know you feel angry. I can see that you are learning to control your anger. That's very good."

2. Tell children that they will not be allowed to hit you or anyone else. Tell them that whenever they hit someone, they will have to go immediately to the "quiet area" for three minutes.

3. From then on, if children hit others, remind them that hitting is not allowed and take them to the "quiet area." Leave them there for three minutes or until they have been quiet for three minutes.

4. Don't say: "Stop that hitting" or "Don't you hit me." You'll only be giving attention to the misbehavior.

5. It is a good thing to reward children when they are first learning not to hit others. If they have shown self-control, praise them as in number 1, above. Tell them they may stay up an extra half hour to watch TV, or give them something they really like.

Adult Dialog

EXAMPLE 1   Praising for not hitting.

(Young boy is building with blocks. His sister walks by and bumps the table. He yells: "Watch out!" His sister says: "What did I do?" He looks at her angrily and starts to hit her. Then he stops, sighs, and says: "Don't you see that I'm building this tower? You bumped the table and almost knocked it over. Please be more careful.")

A: **I'm glad to hear that you are using words instead of fists to settle your quarrels. That shows you are really learning to control your anger. I like that.**

EXAMPLE 2   Setting conditions.

(One child is playing a card game. Another child comes into the room.)

C: Hey! Those are my cards. Who said you could use them?

A: (Sees possibility of a fight.)
If you two can solve your problem with words, we will go over to Grandmother's house after supper.

(Both children grin, then proceed to settle their problem by talking it over.)

A: It's good to hear you settling your quarrel so peacefully. I'll call Grandmother and tell her we're coming.

EXAMPLE 3   Sending to "quiet area" for hitting; noticing good behavior; praising.

(A little girl and her brother are playing together. Suddenly the brother yells: "You cheated!")

C: (Hits brother on the back.)

A: (Quietly goes to child and takes her to "quiet area.")
Hitting is not allowed. You must sit and be quiet for one minute.
(Ignores child for one minute.)
Now you may go and play with your brother.

C: (Plays with brother for one minute without hitting him.)

A: I see you are playing well together. I like cooperation. I think you deserve some lemonade.

INTERRUPTING

In order to break a child's habit of interrupting, follow all of these rules:

1. State the rule: "It is not polite to interrupt when someone is talking. If you wait until the other person is finished, you may speak."

2. If a child waits for you to finish speaking after you have given a reminder, you should say:

"Thank you for waiting. What would you like to say to me?" Give the child your full attention.

3. If a child sees you talking and does *not* interrupt you, give a lot of praise. Be aware of when the child is behaving.

4. Whenever a child interrupts, say quietly: "Please wait until I am finished." Say nothing more. Eventually, just putting your finger to your lips should be enough to remind the child to wait. (CAUTION: Never give in to children's interruptions.)

Adult Dialog

EXAMPLE 1   Stating rules and praising.

A: (Is talking with spouse in living room.)

C: (Bursts in and shouts.) I can't open the peanut butter jar!

A: Wait, please, until we are finished talking. Then one of us will help you.

C: (Goes out quietly and waits.)

A: (Finishes talking.)
Thank you for waiting, Jane. Let's see about that peanut butter jar now.

EXAMPLE 2   Praising for not interrupting.

A: (Is talking to neighbor at kitchen door.)

C: (Comes into kitchen, sees adults talking, and sits quietly at kitchen table.)

A: (Finishes conversation with neighbor.) **Thank you very much for waiting so quietly, Bobby. Would you like to talk to me now?**

C: Can I have something to eat?

A: **Yes, you may. Would you like an apple or an orange?**

EXAMPLE 3   Reminding and ignoring.

A: (Talking on telephone.)

C: Hey! Mom!

A: (Puts finger to lips.)

C: Can I go outside to play?

A: (Ignores child's question.)

C: (Sits down quietly and waits.)

A: (Finishes phone conversation.)
**Thanks for waiting, Cathy. Now, what
would you like to ask me?**

JABBERING

Children who talk too much may be trying to get your attention. On the other hand, they may be nervous and unsure of themselves, and are trying to cover up that fact by jabbering. Some children need a good deal of reassurance. They need to know how much you love them and how important they are to you.

1. If children have difficulty carrying on a conversation, you can teach them. Set aside five to ten minutes a day when you and the child can talk. You begin the conversation, then let the child talk. Take turns. Make sure the child holds up his or her end of the conversation.

2. When a child talks too much, explain that no one likes to be around a person who does all the talking. Say that you will be happy to talk whenever you can have a give-and-take conversation about something worthwhile.

3. When a child does *not* jabber, be sure to give praise. Let the child know that you enjoy his or her company even when there is no conversation.

4. If a child interrupts others, observe the rules in the section on "Interrupting," page 75.

Adult Dialog

EXAMPLE 1   Praising for not talking too much.

C: (Has been quietly fingerpainting for five minutes.)

A: This is really great. You have been working hard and haven't made any noise. I really like that.
(Gives child a hug to go with the praise.)

EXAMPLE 2   Teaching how to work quietly.

C: (Has been following you around the house, jabbering constantly as you are doing your housework.)

A: Jill, if you want to be with me, I'd really appreciate it if you would help. We can work together.

C: (Quietly helps with household chores.)

A: **Thank you, Jill. It's nice to have your help. I really enjoy just being with you. We don't have to talk all the time.**

EXAMPLE 3   Setting conditions; rewarding for not jabbering.

C: Nine. Number nine. Is that the show? Trees. And so there! Blah, blah, telephone, bug, and then, number nine, number nine.

A: **If you sit quietly for one minute, you may do something special that is fun. Let's time it and see if you can do that.**

C: (Sits quietly for one minute.)

A: **That's very good. Do you see how easy it is to be quiet? Let's do something fun.** (Do something that the child really enjoys.)

EXAMPLE 4   Teaching how to have a conversation.

C: (Is jabbering about nothing.)

A: **Let's talk together. I would like to talk about your favorite toy. Which of your toys do you like best?**

C: My teddy bear.

A: **What do you like about your teddy bear?** (Continue to ask questions about the toy, or talk about anything else that appeals to the child.)

SULKING; POUTING; WHINING

Children sulk, pout, or whine to get their own way. This type of behavior continues because children have been reinforced for it. Children remember that when they have sulked, pouted, or whined in the past, they have gotten what they wanted. So the chances are the next time they want something, they will act the same way. Because these behaviors are so similar, they can be handled in much the same way.

1. When children sulk, pout, or whine, ignore them. If you give in just once, you will have

reinforced the behavior and it will appear again.

2. If it is hard for you to ignore whining children, go into another room. Some children actually follow adults from room to room to make sure they are noticed. Ignore such children, and eventually they will give up.

3. Be sure to watch children. When they begin to give up sulking, pouting, or whining, praise them. Say: "I enjoy seeing you happy" or "You're being cheerful today. That makes me cheerful." If children don't sulk or pout when they have been disappointed, tell them how proud you are of them.

   If you are in a situation where children often whine, but don't (such as during dinner when they want dessert), praise them. Say: "Thank you for asking for dessert in a normal voice. I like to hear your normal voice."

Adult Dialog

EXAMPLE 1   Ignoring whining.

C: May I have some pie? Please, please! I want some pie. Please, oh please! I need some pie.

A: It's dinnertime, and you may not have any pie now. If you ask me in a normal voice after dinner, you may have some then.

C: Oh, but I want some pie now. Please? Please!

A: (Ignores child whining. Does not give child any pie before or after dinner. Explains rules to child once, and does not repeat them.)

EXAMPLE 2   Praising for not whining.

C: May I have a cookie?

A: After dinner you may have a cookie. Thank you for talking in your normal voice. Your voice sounds much nicer when you don't whine.
(Give the child a hug, and make sure he or she receives a cookie after dinner.)

EXAMPLE 3   Ignoring whining.

C: I want to stay up late tonight. There's a really good TV show on. Please, Mom! Please let me stay up to watch it.

A: You have to get up early tomorrow to start for camp. You must go to bed at the usual time.

C: Oh, Mom! I *have* to stay up. Please! Please! Let me stay up.

A: (Puts child to bed. Ignores whining and does not refer to it.)

NOTE: Some additional ideas are contained in the section on "Arguing," page 64.

SWEARING

If *you* swear, a child will probably swear. He or she may try out some "forbidden words" in order to enjoy your shocked reaction or in order to appear "grown-up." These suggestions may help you teach children not to swear:

1. Watch children when they are in situations where they *might* swear. If they use another, more acceptable word, praise them for *not* swearing. For example: "I know that you are upset, but I liked the way you expressed it."

2. When children swear, explain that such language is not allowed and suggest that they use more acceptable speech. Each time children use a more acceptable word, praise them.

3. If children still swear after you have told them not to, take them to the "quiet area" right away for one to three minutes. Do this *every time* children swear. Make sure they understand the rule and know why they are going to the "quiet area." Say: "You may not swear" or "You may not use that word!" Do not say anything else.

4. Keep cool. If it appears that children are swearing just to shock you and get your attention, ignore the swearing if there are no other people close by. If there are others around, quietly move children to a "quiet area." Above all, do not allow children to think that they have succeeded in shocking you.

You may have to put children in the "quiet area" more than once. When they finally realize you are serious, they will understand that they must go to the "quiet area" if they swear. If they use a more acceptable word, they will make you happy and receive praise.

Adult Dialog

EXAMPLE 1   Praising for not swearing.

C: That darn Billy hit me again today.

A: **I'm sorry that Billy hit you, but I like the way you said it. Let's go and play a game together.**

C: Okay!

EXAMPLE 2   Teaching child to use another
word.

C: I can't make this damned puzzle fit.

A: **Steven, please don't say that word. I
know you are upset about the puzzle.
But please use a word that is acceptable.**

C: I can't make this crazy puzzle fit.

A: **That's better, Steven. That sounds much
nicer. Now let me see if I can help you
with it.**

EXAMPLE 3   Taking to "quiet area" for
swearing.

C: There isn't a damned thing on television
tonight!

A: **You know the rule. You are not allowed
to swear.**
(Takes child to "quiet area." Explains that he
or she must sit without talking for a certain
period of time. At the end of the time, allow
the child to return to what he or she was
doing.)

THROWING TANTRUMS

A tantrum is a fit of temper in which children cry, stomp their feet, ignore instructions, or act very cross. If children throw tantrums often, it is probably because they have gotten what they wanted by doing so.

1. When children throw tantrums in places where they will not disturb other people, ignore them. You may leave the room. If children follow you, let them know you will not permit that. If no one is around to notice tantrums, children will eventually discover that tantrums will not get them what they want.

2. If you are in public when children throw tantrums, take them out to the car, for instance, and put them in the back seat. You sit in front and say that you are going to sit there until they quiet down. Ignore them. Always stay with children, but give them no attention. When they have finished their tantrums, take them back wherever you were and continue what you were doing.

   You must take children back to where you were, or they might get the idea that they can throw tantrums to make you leave a place. Do not let children keep you away from certain places because of their tantrums. You will probably have to repeat this procedure several times before a child understands that he or she cannot get away with tantrums.

3. If children have tantrums at one particular time or place, you might be able to forstall them by promising to do something afterward that they enjoy. Explain this to a child ahead of time: "We are going to the dentist. If you behave, we will go to the park afterward and you can play on the swings."

Adult Dialog

EXAMPLE 1   Ignoring tantrum.

(You are at home, and you have no visitors. Cecily's tantrum will not disturb anyone else. She is crying and kicking.)

A: (Ignore the child. If the tantrum is getting out of hand and you are having trouble ignoring her, leave the room. Let her cry it out, but do not let her do anything destructive.)

EXAMPLE 2   Taking child to car during tantrum.

(George is crying and having tantrum in supermarket because you will not buy him some candy.)

A: Having a tantrum will not get you what you want.

C: (Continues tantrum.)

A: We are going to go and sit in the car until you can behave. Then we will come back and finish our shopping.
(Takes child out to car and puts him in back seat. Gets in front. Ignores child's tantrum.)

C: (Finally stops crying and fussing.)

A: I see you are ready to behave. Now we can go finish our shopping.
(If the child has another tantrum, repeat the above.)

EXAMPLE 3   Setting conditions.

A: Come, Charles. We are going over to the dress shop.

C: Aw, Mom! It's no fun in that shop. There's nothing to do.

A: I know that you don't enjoy it, but I need to do some shopping. If you behave while we're there, I'll take you to the pet shop afterward to look at the animals.

C: Okay.

TEASING

If children tease other children, it is probably because they enjoy others' reactions and have found that teasing will get them what they want. The child who is being teased is not always innocent. He or she may actually encourage the teasing.

1. When children realize that teasing will not get them what they want, they will stop teasing. As they begin to let up, be sure to praise them. Say: "I like the way you are getting along with others now. You are learning to be nice to people."

2. If children continue to tease after you have admonished them, tell them they will have to go to the "quiet area" every time they tease others. When they stop teasing, remember to praise them.

3. To teach children how to avoid being teased, explain that part of the reason they are teased is because they react to it. Tell children to ignore the teasing—to walk away from teasers. If children are being teased to lend a toy, for instance, tell them to say: "I am playing with this now. You can play with it when I am through."

4. If a child is being teased and ignores it, be sure to give praise. Say: "I like the way you didn't let teasing bother you. You are working very hard at that."

Adult Dialog

EXAMPLE 1   Praising for ignoring teasing and for not teasing.

(Billy is teasing Jean, who is screaming and crying.)

A: (Talks with Jean. Asks her to help teach Billy not to tease. Tells her that when Billy teases, she should ignore him or walk away. Explains that screaming and crying make Billy tease more.)

C: Jean is a sissy! All girls are sissies. Sissy! Sissy!
(Continues to taunt Jean, who pays no attention.)

A: Jean, I like the way you are not paying attention to Billy's teasing.

C: (Stops teasing when he realizes Jean is ignoring him.)

A: It's really nice, Billy, that you have stopped teasing Jean.
(Returns to chores and lets children play alone. When one child ignores teasing and the other stops, praise both children for their actions. You must be sure to work with both children.)

EXAMPLE 2   Taking to "quiet area" for teasing.

C: (To a younger brother.) I get to go to school and you don't. Ha, ha! You have to stay home.

A: You know the rule. You are not allowed to tease.
(Takes child to "quiet area.")
You must sit quietly for two minutes.

EXAMPLE 3   Praising for not teasing.

C: (Is playing with other children and getting along well.)

A: This is really nice. I like to see you getting along so well. I'm so happy to see that you are not teasing.

Let Common Sense Be Your Guide

You need not be a child psychologist or attend numerous classes or seminars in child development in order to work successfully with youngsters. Let common sense be your guide. You know that reward for good behavior is more effective than punishment for misbehavior. You know that you must keep any promise you make to a child. If you try putting yourself in the child's place and try feeling what he or she feels, you will be in a better position to know how to cope. Adults who really care about children have the greatest success with them.

TALLY SHEETS
AND GRAPHS

TALLY SHEET

DATES	MON	TUE	WED	THUR	FRI	SAT	SUN	TOTAL

Number of Times the Behavior Occurs

TALLY SHEET

	DATES	MON	TUE	WED	THUR	FRI	SAT	SUN	TOTAL

Number of Times the Behavior Occurs

GRAPH-BY-DAYS

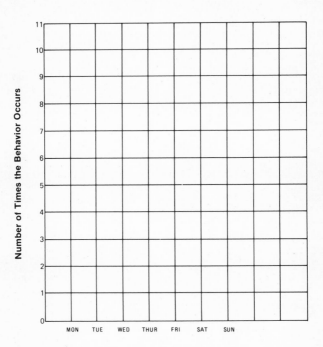

GRAPH-BY-DAYS

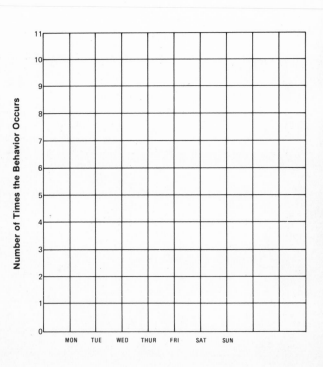

GRAPH-BY-WEEKS

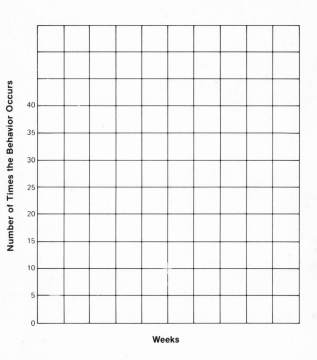

GRAPH-BY-WEEKS

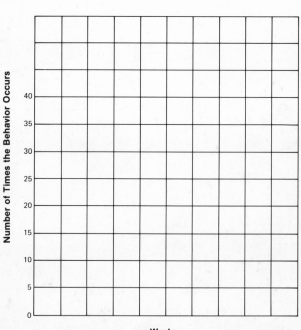

Number of Times the Behavior Occurs

40

35

30

25

20

15

10

5

0

Weeks